DEREK MAHON

LIVES

CHESTER COLLEGE

ACC. No.   DEPT.
131830
CLASS No.
821·914 MAH

LIBRARY

WITHDRAWN

LONDON
OXFORD UNIVERSITY PRESS
1972

Oxford University Press, Ely House, London W.1

GLASGOW NEW YORK TORONTO MELBOURNE WELLINGTON
CAPE TOWN IBADAN NAIROBI DAR ES SALAAM LUSAKA ADDIS ABABA
DELHI BOMBAY CALCUTTA MADRAS KARACHI LAHORE DACCA
KUALA LUMPUR SINGAPORE HONG KONG TOKYO

ISBN 0 19 211816 1

© *Oxford University Press,* 1972

*All rights reserved. No part of this publication may be reproduced,
stored in a retrieval system, or transmitted, in any form or by any
means, electronic, mechanical, photocopying, recording or otherwise,
without the prior permission of Oxford University Press*

*Printed in Great Britain by
The Bowering Press, Plymouth*

For my father and mother

Acknowledgements

Acknowledgements are due to the editors of the following periodicals, in which some of these poems first appeared: *Agenda, Aquarius, Atlantis, Broadsheet, Hibernia, The Honest Ulsterman, Icarus, The Listener, The Malahat Review, New Irish Writing,* and *Threshold,* and to the BBC and Radio Telefís Éireann. Some of the poems have also appeared in pamphlets published by the Phoenix Press, Manchester, and Turret Books. 'Beyond Howth Head' was originally published in pamphlet form by the Dolmen Press, Dublin.

Contents

Homecoming

HAS bath and shave
clean shirt etcetera,
full of potat-
oes, rested, yet
badly distraught
by six-hour flight
(Boston to Dublin)
drunk all night
with crashing bore
from Houston, Tex.,
who spoke at length
on guns and sex.
Bus into town
and, sad to say,
no change from when
he went away
two years ago.
Goes into bar,
affixes gaze
on evening star.
Skies change but not
souls change; behold
this is the way
the world grows old.
Scientists, birds,
we cannot start
at this late date
with a pure heart,
or having seen
the pictures plain
be ever in-
nocent again.

A Dying Art

THAT day would skin a fairy—
A dying art, she said.
Not many left of the old trade.
Redundant and remote, they age
Gracefully in dark corners
With lamplighters, sailmakers
And native Manx speakers.

And the bone-handled knives with which
They earned their bread? My granny grinds
Her plug tobacco with one to this day.

Ecclesiastes

GOD, you could grow to love it, God-fearing, God-
    chosen purist little puritan that,
for all your wiles and smiles, you are (the
    dank churches, the empty streets,
the shipyard silence, the tied-up swings) and
    shelter your cold heart from the heat
of the world, from woman-inquisition, from the
    bright eyes of children. Yes you could
wear black, drink water, nourish a fierce zeal
    with locusts and wild honey, and not
feel called upon to understand and forgive
    but only to speak with a bleak
afflatus, and love the January rains when they
    darken the dark doors and sink hard
into the Antrim hills, the bog meadows, the heaped
    graves of your fathers. Bury that red
bandana and stick, that banjo, this is your
    country, close one eye and be king.
Your people await you, their heavy washing
    flaps for you in the housing estates—
a credulous people. God, you could do it, God
    help you, stand on a corner stiff
with rhetoric, promising nothing under the sun.

Edvard Munch

You would think with so much going on outside
The deal table would make for the window,
The ranged crockery freak and wail
Remembering its dark origins, the frail
Oilcloth, in a fury of recognitions,
Disperse in a thousand directions,
And the simple bulb in the ceiling, honed
By death to a worm of pain, to a hair
Of heat, to a light snowflake laid
In a dark river at night—and wearied
Above all by the life-price of time
And the failure by only a few tenths
Of an inch but completely and for ever
Of the ends of a carefully drawn equator
To meet, sing and be one—abruptly
Roar into the floor.
                                But it
Never happens like that. Instead
There is this quivering silence
In which, day by day, the play
Of light and shadow (shadow mostly)
Repeats itself, though never exactly.

This is the all-purpose bed-, work- and bedroom.
Its mourning faces are cracked porcelain only quicker,
Its knuckles door-knobs only lighter,
Its occasional cries of despair
A function of the furniture.

In the Aran Islands

He is earthed to his girl, one hand fastened
In hers, and with his free hand listens,
An earphone, to his own rendition,
Singing the darkness into the light.
I close the pub door gently and step out
Into the yard, and the song goes out
And a gull creaks off from the corrugated
Iron roof of an outhouse, over the ocean,
Circling now with a hoarse inchoate
Screaming the boned fields of its vision.
God, that was the way to do it,
Hand-clasping, echo-prolonging poet.

Scorched with a fearful admiration
Walking over the nacreous sand,
I dream myself to that tradition,
Fifty winters off the land —
One hand to an ear for the vibration,
The far wires, the reverberation
Down light-years of the imagination
And, in the other hand, your hand.

The long glow leaps from the dark soil, however—
No marshlight holds a candle to this.
Unearthly still in its white weather
A crack-voiced rock-marauder, scavenger, fierce
Friend to no slant fields or the sea either,
Folds back over the forming waters.

Rocks

THE rocks would never recognize
The image of themselves
These lovers entertain,
Lying in their shadows
In the last traces of time.

All they know is their own
Shuddering endurance,
Their dream of holding fast
In the elemental flux—
Bewildered both in the
Approach and the discovery.

Night Song

MONTHS on, you hold me still;
at dawn, bright-rising, like a hill-
horizon, gentle, kind with rain
and the primroses of April.
I shall never know them again
but still your bright shadow
puts out its shadow, daylight, on
the shadows I lie with now.

An Image from Beckett

for Doreen Douglas

IN that instant
There was a sea, far off,
As bright as lettuce,

A northern landscape
(Danish?) and a huddle of
Houses along the shore.

Also, I think,
A white flicker of gulls and
Washing hung to dry—

The poignancy of those
Back yards—and the gravedigger
Putting aside his forceps.

Then the hard boards
And darkness once again.
Oh, I might have proved

So many heroes!
Sorel, perhaps, or
Kröger, given the time.

For in that instant
I was struck by the sweetness and light,
The sweetness and light,

Imagining what grave
Cities, what lasting monuments,
Given the time.

8

But even my poor house
I left unfinished;
And my one marriage

Was over as soon as it started,
Its immanence so brief as to be
Immeasurable.

They will have buried
My great-grandchildren, and theirs,
Beside me by now

With a subliminal
Batsqueak of reflex lamentation.
Our hair and excrement

Litter the rich earth
Changing, second by second,
To civilizations.

It was good while it lasted;
And if it only lasted
The Biblical span

Required to drop six feet
Through a glitter of wintry light,
There is No-one to blame.

Still, I am haunted
By that landscape,
The soft rush of its winds,

The uprightness of its
Utilities and schoolchildren—
To whom in my will,

This, I have left my will.
I hope they had time, and light
Enough, to read it.

The Last Dane

for Tom and Peggy MacIntyre

HE had seen in dreams the place where he would die—
Mirrors, cushions, a light-switch
Quick and predictable to the touch,
Re-bound first editions; but left instead

From the last island on the furthest sea-board,
No mirror but the sea,
Stones for a pillow, self-knowledge for a bed,
A home-made handloom for technology.

What last word, what precept or example
For the belt-buying people? Dying
He left us these for their simplicity—
A knife, a loaf of bread,
A milk-jug and a half-empty mug of tea.

The Archaeologist

for Hugh Maxton

THROUGH heaving heather, fallen stones
From the wrecked piles of burial cairns
As they fly in over the moors—
Racing about in cloud-shadow,
A stone-age figure far below
Wildly gesticulating as if
He sees, at last, a sign of life
Or damns them to hell-fires.

When they come with poles, binoculars, whistles,
Blankets and flasks, they will find him dead—
Unkempt, authentic, furnace-eyed and
Dead, and his heavy flint hearthstones
Littered with dung and animal bones;

Or a local resident out for a walk
In tweeds and a hunting hat. You must be
Mad, he will say, to suppose this rock
Could accommodate life indefinitely;
Nobody comes here now but me.

J. P. Donleavy's Dublin

WHEN you stop to consider
The days spent dreaming of a future
And say then, that was my life.

For the days are long—
From the first milk-van
To the last shout in the night,
An eternity. But the weeks go by
Like birds; and the years, the years
Fly past anti-clockwise
Like clock-hands in a bar mirror.

Lives

FIRST time out
I was a torc of gold
And wept tears of the sun.

That was fun but
They buried me in the
Earth two thousand years

Till a labourer
Turned me up with a pick
In eighteen fifty-four

And sold me for
Tea and sugar in
Newmarket-on-Fergus.

Once I was an oar
But stuck in the shore
To mark the place of a grave

When the lost fleet
Sailed away. I thought of
Carthage but soon withered.

The time that I
Liked best was when
I was a bump of clay

In a Navaho rug,
Put there to mitigate
The too godlike

14

Perfection of that
Merely human artefact.
I served my maker well—

He lived long
To be struck down in
Tucson by an electric shock

The night the
Lights went out in Europe
Never to shine again.

So many lives,
So many things to remember!
I was a stone in Tibet,

A tongue of bark
At the heart of Africa
Growing darker and darker ...

It all seems
A little unreal now,
Now that I am

An anthropologist
With my own
Credit card, dictaphone,

Army-surplus boots
And a whole boatload
Of photographic equipment.

I know too much
To be anything any more—
And if in the distant

Future someone
Thinks he has once been me
As I am today,

Let him revise
His insolent ontology
Or teach himself to pray.

Deaths

Who died nails, key-rings
Sword hilts and lunulae
Rose hash, bog-paper
And deciduous forests
Died again these things

Rose kites, wolves
Piranha fish and bleached
To a white femur
By desert by dark river

Fight now for our
Fourth lives with an
Informed, articulate
Fury frightening to the
Unreflecting progenitors

Who crowd our oxygen tents.
What should we fear
Who never lost by dying?
What should we not as

Gunsmiths, botanists, having
Taken the measure of
Life, death, we comb our
Bright souls for
Whatever the past holds?

A Dark Country

STARTING again
After a long patience,
A long absence, is a slow
Riding of undertow,
A ship turning among buoys in dawn rain
To slide into a dockyard fluorescence;

Is a coming
Into a dark country
Beyond appraisal or report
The shape of the human heart.
You will go as you came, a twist of spring
Water through ferns, as febrile and as wintry;

But now move—
Circumspectly at first
But with a growing sense
Of the significance,
Crippling and ordering, of what you love,
Its unique power to create and assuage thirst—

Among these
Signs, these wild declivities
That have in the past
Betrayed you to a waste
Of rage, self-pity bordering on self-hate,
A blind man without comfort at the gate;

Recognizing,
As in a sunken city
Sea-changed at last, the surfaces
Of once familiar places.
With practice you might decipher the whole thing
Or enough to suffer the relief and the pity.

Folk Song

from the Irish

A HUNDRED men imagine
love when I drink wine,
and then I begin to think
of your words and mine.
The mountain is silent now
under a white rush
of snow, and my love like sloe-
blossom on a blackthorn bush.

A Tolerable Wisdom

You keep the cold from the body, the cold from the mind—
heartscloth, soulswool, without you there would be
short shrift for the pale beast in a winter's wind,
too swift exposure by too brute a sea.
Cold I have kown, its sports-pages adrift
past frozen dodgems in the amusement park,
one crumpled Gauloise touting for a lift
where Paris flamed on the defining dark.
You've heard the gravel at the window, seen
a lost figure unmanned by closing-time—
more honour to you that you took him in,
fed buns and cocoa, sweetness, the sought dream
of warmth and light against your listening skin
and rocked him to a tolerable wisdom.

Job's Comforter

You too, cold once, have cried disconsolately
to the dumb mountain so the ravens flew.
Job's saviour, who can save you with his pity?
Job's comforter, who is to comfort you?
Insomniac in the kitchen while Job snores
content and ignorant, do you sometimes hear,
conch-like, a groan of water on the shores
of lives unlived or lived beyond all fear?
Yes, and there love makes its interstices,
hunger the mother of love as of history, art . . .
We die, as we dream, alone. Peace to the places
I can't go with you when the bad dreams start—
stony repositories of hands and faces,
the blind eyes infinitely beyond comfort.

Rage for Order

SOMEWHERE beyond
The scorched gable end
And the burnt-out
Buses there is a poet indulging his
Wretched rage for order—

Or not as the
Case may be, for his
Is a dying art,
An eddy of semantic scruple
In an unstructurable sea.

He is far
From his people,
And the fitful glare
Of his high window is as
Nothing to our scattered glass.

His posture is
Grandiloquent and
Deprecating, like this,
His diet ashes,
His talk of justice and his mother

The rhetorical
Device of a Claudian emperor—
Nero if you prefer,
No mother there;
And this in the face of love, death and the wages of the poor.

If he is silent
It is the silence
Of enforced humility,
If anxious to be heard
It is the anxiety of a last word

When the drums start—
For his is a dying art.
Now watch me
As I make history,
Watch as I tear down

To build up
With a desperate love,
Knowing it cannot be
Long now till I have need of his
Germinal ironies.

After Cavafy

It is night
And the barbarians have not come.
It was not always so hard;
When the great court flared
With gallowglasses and language difficulty
A man could be a wheelwright and die happy.

We remember
Oatmeal and mutton,
Harpsong, a fern table for
Wiping your hands on,
A candle of reeds and butter,
The distaste of the rheumatic chronicler,

A barbarous tongue
And herds like cloud-shadow
Roaming the wet hills
When the hills were young,
Whiskery pikemen and their spiky dogs
Preserved in woodcuts and card-catalogues.

Now it is night
And the barbarians have not come.
Or if they have we only recognize,
Harsh as a bombed bathroom,
The frantic anthropologisms
And lazarous ironies

Behind their talk
Of fitted carpets, central
Heating and automatic gear-change—
Like the bleached bones of a hare
Or a handful of spent
Cartridges on a deserted rifle range.

As It Should Be

WE hunted the mad bastard
Through bog, moorland, rock, to the starlit west
And gunned him down in a blind yard
Between ten sleeping lorries
And an electricity generator.

Let us hear no idle talk
Of the moon in the Yellow River;
The air blows softer since his departure.

Since his tide-burial during school-hours
Our kiddies have known no bad dreams.
Their cries echo lightly along the coast.

This is as it should be.
They will thank us for it when they grow up
To a world with method in it.

What Will Remain

WHAT will remain after
The twilight of metals,
The flowers of fire,

Will be the soft
Vegetables where our
Politics were conceived.

It is hard not to imagine
What it must have been like
Before any of us were here

And to what dark
Repose it will in time return.
When we give back

The cleared counties to the
First forest, the hills
To the hills, the reclaimed

Mudflats to the vigilant sea,
What will remain will be
The blank nature before

Whiskey, before scripture,
Its white lakes at one
With the skies' reflection,

One hare on the horizon,
One dog rooting the
Red guts of another

Where a new ploughshare factory
Was opened today,
An eagle at its liver
Where we are filming now—

As if, without ideas, they too
Moved in a slow dance
Of the purest energy,

Intent on a reiterative
Exercise of known powers
Under the mineral stars.

Consolations of Philosophy

for Eugene Lambe

WHEN we start breaking up in the wet darkness
And the rotten boards fall from us, and the ribs
Crack under the constriction of tree-roots
And the seasons slip from the fields unknown to us

Oh, then there will be the querulous complaining
From citizens who had never dreamed of this—
Who, shaken to the bone in their stout boxes
By the latest bright cars, will not inspect them

And, kept awake by the tremors of new building,
Will not be there to comment. When the broken
Wreath bowls are speckled with rain water
And the grass grows wild for want of a caretaker

Oh, then a few will remember with affection
Dry bread, mousetrap cheese, and the satisfaction
Of picking long butts from a wet gutter
Like daisies from a clover field in summer.

Gipsies Revisited

for Julian Harvey

SORRY, gippos—I have
watched the dark police
rocking your caravans
to wreck the crockery
and wry thoughts of peace
you keep there on waste
ground beside motorways
where the snow lies late
and am ashamed—fed,
clothed, housed and ashamed.
You might be interested
to hear, though, that on
stormy nights our strong
double glazing groans with
foreknowledge of death,
the fridge with a great wound,
and not surprised to know
the fate you have so long
endured is ours also,
the cars are piling up.
I listen to the wind
and file receipts. The heap
of scrap metal in my
garden grows daily.

Entropy

WE are
Holing up here
In the difficult places—

In caves,
Terminal moraines
And abandoned farmhouses,

The wires cut,
The old Citroën
Disposing itself for

Death among
The inscrutable,
Earth-inheriting dandelions.

The roads at
Evening glitter with
Ditched bicycles,

At morning with
The bronze shards
Of a monumental sculptor

Who lived
In the big house before
Being bought out

By a property speculator
Who failed O-levels, O
Time thy pyramids . . .

We are
Hiding out here
With the old methods—

Growing our own,
Chasing hares in the rough.
We are not quick enough

Having become
Heavy and slow from
Long urban idling.

We have tried
To worship the sun,
To make gods of clay,

Gods of stone,
But gave up in derision.
We have pared life to the bone

And squat now
In the firelight reading
Gibbon and old comics.

Somewhere
The old folks dream on,
Their innocence and purpose

A twig, a leaf
Eddying in brown
Discrepancies of water

While we,
Anemones, receive
On our bare rock

Whatever
Nourishment the wash
Of the waves may bring.

I Am Raftery

I AM Raftery, hesitant and confused among the
cold-voiced graduate students and inter-
changeable instructors. Were it not for the
nice wives who do the talking I would have
run out of hope some time ago, and of love.
I have traded in the simplistic maunderings
that made me famous for a wry dissimulation,
an imagery of adventitious ambiguity dredged
from God knows what polluted underground spring.
Death is near, I have come of age, I doubt if
I shall survive another East Anglian winter.
Scotch please, plenty of water. I am reading
Joyce in braille and it's killing me. Is it
empty pockets I play to? Not on your life,
they ring with a bright inflationary music—
two seminars a week and my own place reserved
in the record library. Look at me now,
my back to the wall, taking my cue from a
grinning disc-jockey between commercials.

Beyond Howth Head

*Il faut parier. Cela n'est pas
volontaire; vous êtes embarqué.*
Pascal, *Pensées*

for Jeremy Lewis

THE wind that blows these words to you
bangs nightly off the black-and-blue
Atlantic, hammering in its haste
dark doors of the declining west
whose rock-built houses year by year
collapse, whose strong sons disappear
(no homespun cottage industries'
embroidered cloths will patch up these

lost townlands on the crumbling shores
of Europe); shivers the thin stars
in rain water; and spins a single
garage sign behind the shingle.
Fresh from Long Island or Cape Cod
night music finds the lightning rod
of 'young girls coming from a dance'
(you thumbs a lift and takes your chance)

and shakes the radio sets that play
from the Twelve Pins to Dublin Bay
where, in contempt of Telefís,
vox populi vox dei, we reach
with twinkling importunity
for good news on the BBC,
our heliotropic Birnam Wood
reflecting an old gratitude.

33

What can the elders say to this?
For girls must kiss and then must kiss
and so by this declension fall
to write the writing on the wall.
A little learning in a parked
Volkswagen torches down the dark
and soon disperses fogged Belief
with an empiric *joie de vivre*.

The pros outweigh the cons that glow
from Beckett's bleak *reductio*;
and who would trade self-knowledge for
a prelapsarian metaphor,
love-play of the ironic conscience
for a prescriptive innocence?
'Lewde libertie', whose midnight work
disturbed the peace of Co. Cork

and fired Kilcolman's windows when
the flower of Ireland looked to Spain,
come back and be with us again!
But take a form that sheds for love
that tight-arsed, convent-bred disdain
the whole wide world knows nothing of
and flash, an *aisling*, through the dawn
where Yeats's hill-men still break stone.

The writing on the wall, we know,
elsewhere was written long ago.
We fumble with the light-switch while
the hebona behind the smile
of grammar gets its brisk forensic
smack in the *realpolitik*
and Denmark's hot stylistics pass
to the cool courts of Cambridge, Mass.,

leaving us, Jeremy, to flick
blank pages of an empty book
where the 'outdated futures' lie
wide to the runways and the sky;
to spin celestial globes of words
over a foaming pint in Ward's,
bent victims of our linear thought
(though booze is *bourgeois* pot is not)

rehearsing for the *fin de siècle*
gruff Jeremiads to redirect
lost youth into the knacker's yard
of humanistic self-regard;
to praise what will be taken from us,
the Spartan code of Dylan Thomas;
and sign off with a pounding pen
from Cheltenham or Inishmaan.

I woke this morning (March) to hear
church bells of Monkstown through the roar
of waves round the Martello tower
and thought of the swan-sons of Lir
when Kemoc rang the Christian bell
to crack a fourth-dimensional
world-picture, never known again,
and changed them back from swans to men.

It calls as oddly through the wild
eviscerations of the troubled
channel between us and North Wales
where Lycid's ghost for ever sails
(unbosomings of sea-weed, wrack,
industrial bile, a boot from Black-
pool, contraceptives deftly tied
with best regards from Merseyside)

and tinkles with as blithe a sense
of man's cosmic significance
who wrote his world from broken stone,
installed his Word-God on the throne
and placed, in Co. Clare, a sign:
'Stop here and see the sun go down'.
Meanwhile, for a word's sake, the plast-
ic bombs go off around Belfast;

from an Aegean prison now
a Greek poet consults the sky
where sleepless, cold, computed stars
in random sequence light the bars;
and the United States, whose swell
intentions pave the road to hell,
send in the CIA to make
Cambodia safe for Dick Van Dyke.

Oh, everywhere the ground is thick
with the dead sparrows rhetoric
demands as fictive sacrifice
to prove its substance in our eyes.
Roaring, its ten-lane highways pitch
their simple bodies in the ditch
(where once Molloy, uncycled, heard
thin cries of a surviving bird)—

dissolving once again, it seems,
our fond amelioristic dreams
to loss is gain and gain is loss,
cracked spectacles of poor Pangloss;
snow still in the Tsar's room where Lenin rushed in from the hissing train
and snow-reflected sunlight where
an old world crossed the Delaware.

Spring lights the country: from a thous-
and dusty corners, house by house,
from under beds and vacuum cleaners,
empty Kosangas containers,
bread bins, car seats, crates of stout,
the first flies cry to be let out;
to cruise a kitchen, find a door
and die clean in the open air

whose smokeless clarity distils
a chisel's echo in the hills,
as if some Noah, weather-wise,
could read a deluge in clear skies;
but nothing ruffles the wind's breath.
This peace is the sweet peace of death
or *l'outre-tombe*. Make no noise,
the foxes have quit Clonmacnois.

I too, uncycled, might exchange
(since 'we are changed by what we change')
my forkful of the general mess
for hazel nuts and water cress
like one of those old hermits who,
less virtuous than some, withdrew
from the world-circles women make
to a small island in a lake.

Chomei at Toyama, his blank-
et hemp, his character a rank
not-to-be-trusted river mist,
events in Kyoto all grist
to the mill of a harsh irony,
since we are seen by what we see;
Thoreau like ice among the trees;
and Spenser, 'farre from enemyes',

might serve as models for a while
but to return in greater style.
Centripetal, the hot world draws
its children in with loving claws
from rock and heather, rain and sleet
with only Kosangas for heat
and spins them at the centre where
they have no time to know despair

but still, like Mrs Fuller, must
'accept the universe' on trust
and offer to a phantom future
blood and ouns in forfeiture—
each one, his poor loaf on the sea,
monstrous before posterity,
his micro-fury turning brown
and dying ,as we dream, alone.

The light that left you streaks the walls
of Georgian houses, pubs, cathedrals,
coasters moored below Butt Bridge
and old men at the water's edge
where Anna Livia, breathing free,
weeps silently into the sea,
her small sorrows mingling with
the wandering waters of the earth;

and here I close my *Dover Beach*
scenario, for look! the watch-
ful Baily winks beyond Howth Head,
my *cailín bán* lies snug in bed
and the moon rattles the lost stones
among the rocks and the strict bones
of the drowned as I put out the light
on Mailer's *Armies of the Night*.

March–April, **1970**

Notes to *Beyond Howth Head*

To you. The poem was conceived as a letter, from Dublin, to a friend in London.

Embroidered cloths. Yeats: 'Aedh Wishes for the Cloths of Heaven'.

Birnam Wood. Television aerials.

Lewde libertie. In Spenser's *Veue of the Present State of Irelande*. He lived at Kilcolman Castle, Co. Cork, burnt in 1598.

Aisling. 'Vision'; more particularly, a vision of a young woman symbolizing Irish freedom, as in the poems of Egan O'Rahilly (1670-1726). Pronounced *ash-ling*.

Still break stone. Yeats: 'Parnell came down the road, he said to a cheering man: Ireland shall get her freedom and you still break stone.'

Hebona. The poison used by Claudius to kill Hamlet's father. One may smile and smile and be a villain.

Cambridge, Mass. Harvard and MIT.

Outdated futures. Cohn-Bendit: *Obsolete Communism*.

Ward's. An Irish pub in Shaftesbury Avenue.

A sign. For tourists. What it actually says is 'See the sunset from here'.

A Greek poet. No one in particular, although the composer Mikis Theodorakis was still behind bars at this time.

Cambodia. This refers to the deposition of Prince Sihanouk.

Sparrows. Matthew x.29.

Molloy. In the novel by Beckett.

Pangloss. 'All for the best in the best of all possible worlds.'

Lenin. The scene is described by Edmund Wilson in *To the Finland Station*.

Foxes. A ninth-century Irish poem tells how foxes fed on human corpses after the Danes sacked Clonmacnois.

We are changed. Auden: 'New Year Letter'.

Chomei. The twelfth-century Japanese poet. Cf. 'Chomei at Toyama' in Basil Bunting's *Collected Poems*.

Mrs Fuller. The actress.

    Mrs F: 'I accept the universe!'

    Carlyle: 'Madam, you'd better.'

Cailín bán. Fair young woman.

Accession no   LG
732830   01

ISSUE LABEL

**DURATION OF LOAN—Not later than the latest
date stamped below.**

2 6 MAR 19

WITHDRAWN

1 6 MAY 2006